Decision for the Ages

Dr. Stephens

Illustrated by Pamela Mills

To order additional copies of this book, contact
Toll Free +65 3165 7531 (Singapore)
Toll Free +60 3 3099 4412 (Malaysia)
www.partridgepublishing.com/singapore
orders.singapore@partridgepublishing.com

Because of the dynamic nature of the Internet, any web addresses or links contained in this book may have changed since publication and may no longer be valid. The views expressed in this work are solely those of the author and do not necessarily reflect the views of the publisher, and the publisher hereby disclaims any responsibility for them.

ISBN
ISBN: 978-1-5437-7270-8 (sc)
ISBN: 978-1-5437-7272-2 (hc)
ISBN: 978-1-5437-7271-5 (e)

Library of Congress Control Number: 2023900138

Print information available on the last page.

01//13/2023

PARTRIDGE

Lloyd and Jenny sat on their sun porch, looking out over their well-manicured yard on beautiful Lake Murray. They had decades of memories in their home – entertaining friends, hosting festive family holiday gatherings, the day-to-day hustles and bustles of work, and the serene moments that add balance to life.

As much as they loved their home, they wondered how much longer they would be able to live there. Lloyd's mind was not what it used to be. Recently, he realized he had paid some of his bills twice. About a month ago, he had received a call from the electric company to let him know he had forgotten to sign a check that he had mailed for bill payment. At the same time, Jenny's mobility was not what it once had been.

After their retirement, she and Lloyd had basked in the pleasures of carefree days, going on bus tours to places they had always wanted to travel and spending time at their cabin in the mountains. But one day, their retirement dreams came to a frightening halt.

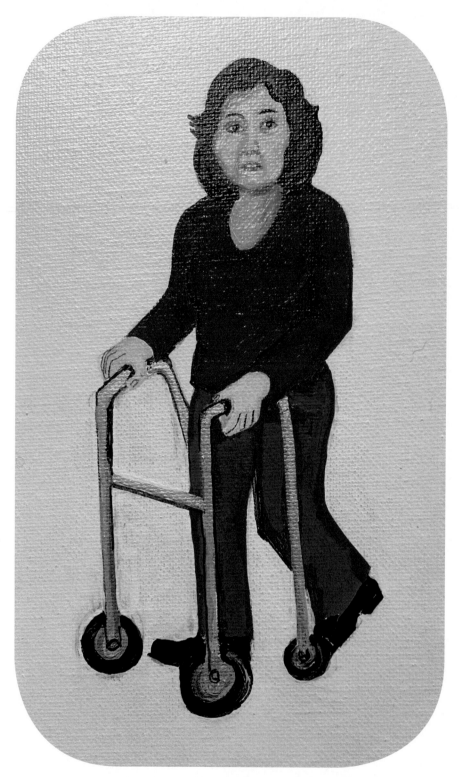

Jenny was out shopping when she suddenly hit the ground. She had suffered a severe stroke. After fighting for her life and months of every type of therapy imaginable, she now relied on the use of a walker and could no longer do many of the activities she had done before – like keep up the house and work in the kitchen to create delicious meals.

Lloyd did the grocery shopping now and prepared items that were easy for him, things like peanut butter and crackers. Though they missed their home-cooked meals, they did not want to give up all the other comforts of home that they had known for decades.

Jenny and Lloyd's living situation
had not gone unnoticed by their
adult children, Angela and Mitch. They
talked between themselves about their
parents' hardships living at home. Mitch
began helping his father with tasks
like yard work and paperwork, while
Angela sometimes prepared meals
for them and did laundry. They
did everything they could
to help them stay in
their home. Yet, they
worried about
their safety and
well-being.

Driving to the grocery store one day, Lloyd became confused and didn't know how to find his way back home. He managed to call Mitch and give him enough information so that he was able to find him. That was an emotional day for them both because they knew that a huge chunk of Lloyd's independence was being ripped from him, and his life would never be the same again. He could not risk his own life and the lives of others. He would have to give up driving.

Mitch phoned Angela the next day to talk about their parents' situation. Neither of them knew what to do, and the call ended with Mitch suggesting that they pray about it.

A decision for the ages needed to be made. It was clear that Lloyd and Jenny could not safely and comfortably live in their home alone. If they were to stay there, they would need someone to come in and prepare meals for them, as well as keep up the day-to-day needs of running the home and tending to their needs.

When Angela and Mitch talked to their parents about having someone come into their home to help them, they said they did not like the idea of someone having access to their personal belongings and private life. They also made it clear that they did not want to be a burden on their children. Mitch and Angela had their own lives and families. It wouldn't be right for them to leave their families and come "back home" and live with their parents.

And...Lloyd and Jenny definitely did not want to move in with either of their children. Not only would moving in with their children disrupt their children's lives, but it would also take away their own privacy and independence. That left only one alternative – finding a suitable place for them to live where they could be happy and get the care they needed

Finding a place for
an elderly couple to live
was new territory for Angela
and Mitch. They remembered
the nursing homes where their
grandmothers had lived in
their advancing years, but
they knew their parents
would not be happy
leaving their home
and going to

such a place.
While they
prayed about it, they
also remembered what
their parents had always told
them, "God helps those who
help themselves." With that advice
in mind, Angela began to search
for information about nearby
quality places for their
parents to live.

She came upon a
nationwide service that offered
recommendations for "children"
in search of a place for their
elderly parents. The service was
free of charge. So, there
was nothing to lose in
contacting them to
see what they might
advise.

The senior care advisor at the nationwide service told Angela about options for senior living. There was Independent Living, Assisted Living, Skilled Nursing, Memory Care, and even Continuing Care Retirement Communities. They had no idea there were so many different types of place for seniors to live!

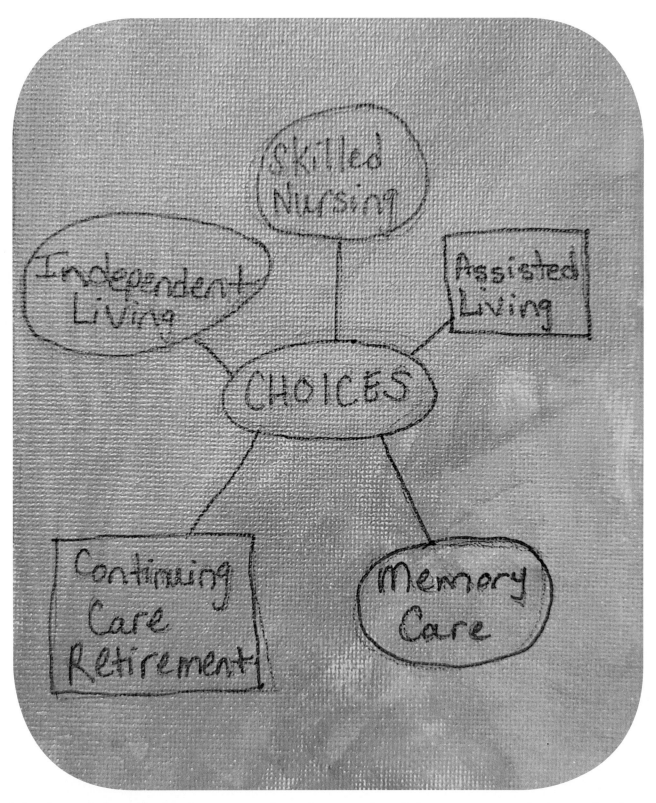

Mitch and Angela had to consider what each of these types of places had to offer, as well as costs and avenues of payment. It was also important to read customer/family reviews and research accreditation reports and other ratings.

Having the assistance of a senior living advisor with information about a huge national network of senior living communities made the task of finding the best place for their parents so much easier than if they had set out on this quest alone. It also gave them confidence and peace of mind about the decision.

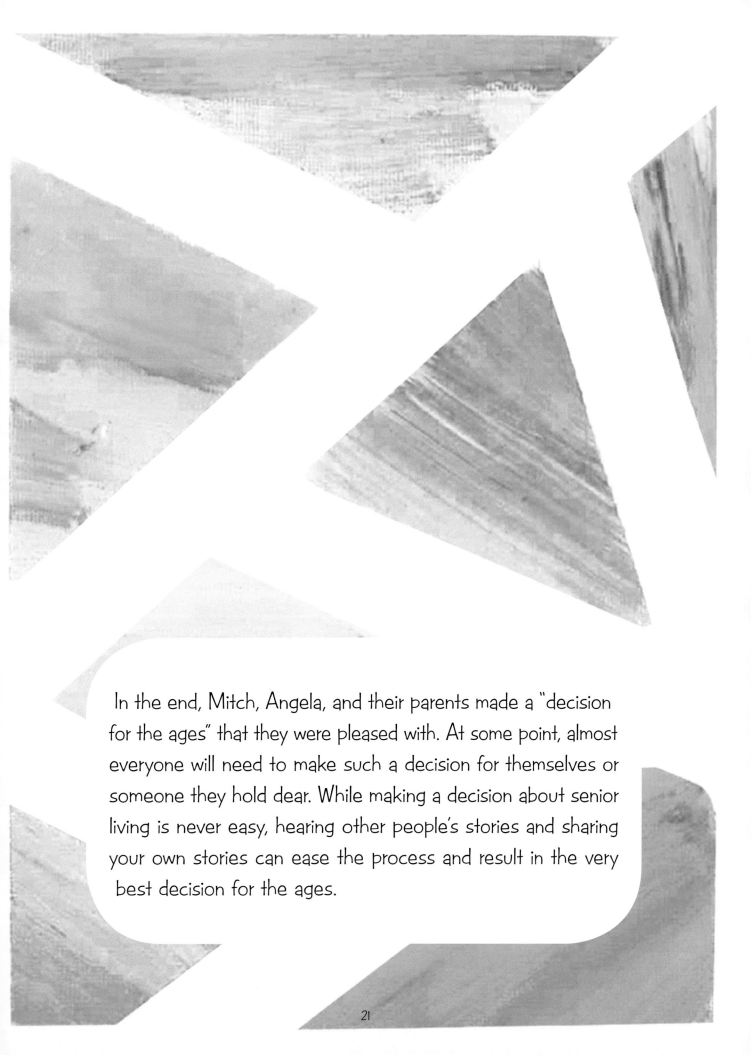

In the end, Mitch, Angela, and their parents made a "decision for the ages" that they were pleased with. At some point, almost everyone will need to make such a decision for themselves or someone they hold dear. While making a decision about senior living is never easy, hearing other people's stories and sharing your own stories can ease the process and result in the very best decision for the ages.

Guiding Questions for Book Discussion

1. Where did you live prior to moving to ___? (Question for those who have moved to a senior living facility) [See page 1]

2. What kinds of activities did you enjoy doing in your home before moving to a senior living facility? (Question for those who have moved to a senior living facility) What kinds of activities do you enjoy doing in your home now? (For those who still live in their home) [See page 1]

3. Tell about a memorable activity that you have done in your senior years? [See page 4]

4. What kinds of activities do you wish you could do in your senior years? For example, would you like to travel somewhere? [See page 4]

5. In Lloyd's case, his dementia hindered him from living at home without help. In Jenny's case, her mobility issues hindered her from living at home without assistance. Do you have any issues that may keep you from living in your home that you would like to share? [See page 6]

6. If you still live in your home, do you have anyone who helps you in your home or in the yard? If you no longer live in your home, did you have someone who helped you in your home/yard before you moved to a senior care facility? [See page 8]

7. How did you go about making decisions for where and how you would spend your senior years? Or, if you have not yet made decisions about where and how you will spend your senior years, how will you go about making these decisions? [See page 13]

8. Do you think it is better to make decisions about how you will spend your senior years while you are young and in good health? [See pages 14-16]

9. Do you want to make your own decisions about how you will spend your senior years, or would you prefer for someone else to make these decisions for you? [See page 21]

10. If for some reason you could not make decisions for yourself about how you will spend your senior years, who would you want to make these decisions? [See page 21]

11. If you do not have a plan in place for aging, would you like to make one today? [End of book]

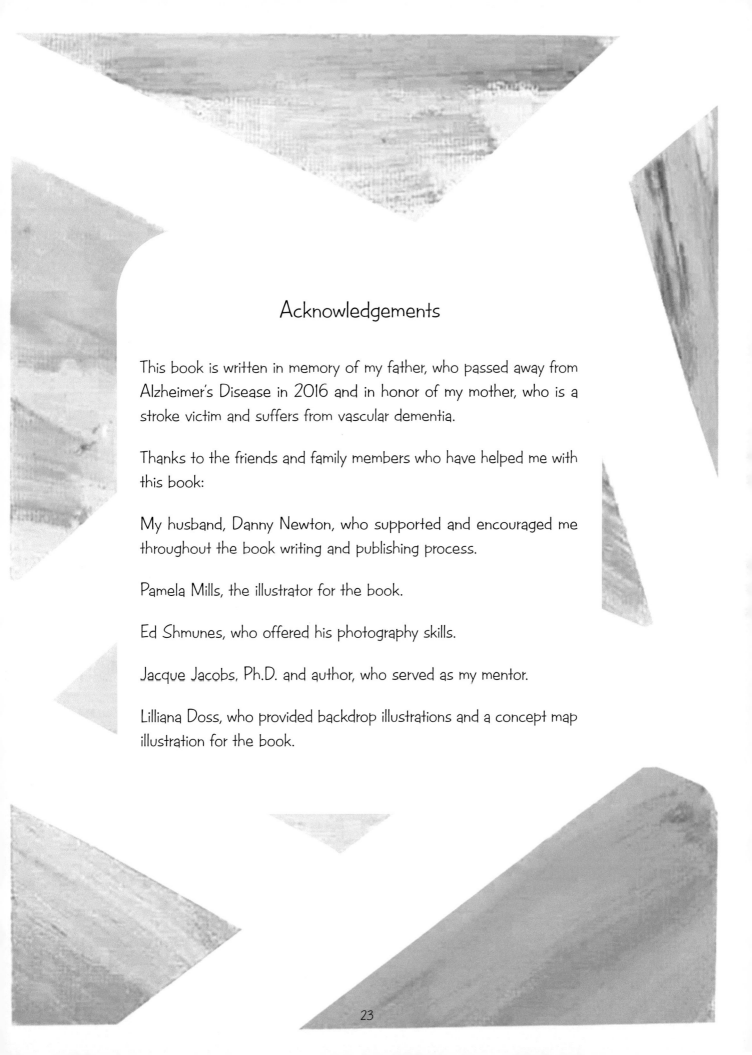

Acknowledgements

This book is written in memory of my father, who passed away from Alzheimer's Disease in 2016 and in honor of my mother, who is a stroke victim and suffers from vascular dementia.

Thanks to the friends and family members who have helped me with this book:

My husband, Danny Newton, who supported and encouraged me throughout the book writing and publishing process.

Pamela Mills, the illustrator for the book.

Ed Shmunes, who offered his photography skills.

Jacque Jacobs, Ph.D. and author, who served as my mentor.

Lilliana Doss, who provided backdrop illustrations and a concept map illustration for the book.

Printed in the United States
by Baker & Taylor Publisher Services